I LOVE BEING ME

Visit our website at www.skyponypress.com.

10 9 8 7 6 5 4 3 2 1

Manufactured in China, January 2021
This product conforms to CPSIA 2008

Library of Congress Cataloging-in-Publication Data is available on file.

Text by Poppy O'Neill
Interior and cover design by Summersdale Publishers Ltd.

Print ISBN: 978-1-5107-6409-5

Printed in China

I LOVE BEING ME

A Child's Guide to Embracing Individuality

Poppy O'Neill

Sky Pony Press
New York

♥ CONTENTS ♥

FOREWORD

Amanda Ashman-Wymbs, Counselor and Psychotherapist, registered and accredited by the British Association for Counseling and Psychotherapy

Having raised two girls and working in schools and the private sector with children for many years, it has become very clear that many children at this time are suffering greatly in their lives from a lack of self-worth. There are many pressures on children today that can affect a child's value of themselves, and with a loss of positive connection to who they are, the child can end up feeling very low, lonely, and unconfident.

This much-needed guide and self-help workbook *I Love Being Me*, by Poppy O'Neill is a great resource to help support children in developing a stronger, healthier relationship with themselves. It offers clear positive affirmations throughout the book and is set up in a way that is appealing to the child, with a friendly monster to join them on the journey. It is full of fun activities that the child works on at their own pace either with or without their parent/caregiver.

The exercises and text in the book support the child's self-awareness and self-acceptance, as they develop an understanding of themselves and others. They will learn what ideas and beliefs are holding them back, and the empathetic style of the book shows them that their experiences and feelings are normal, and that they are not alone. Most importantly, they learn to respect and honor their own and others' uniqueness.

While working through this practical and effective book, the child will experientially develop an insightful and supportive approach to themselves by learning to feel and know the value of being true to who they are. As their perspective and understanding of themselves shifts, their self-esteem will grow, and they will form new positive habits that will resource them for the rest of their lives.

INTRODUCTION: A GUIDE FOR PARENTS AND CAREGIVERS

You're not the only one

All children—and a lot of adults!—struggle to be their true selves sometimes. It can be really tough to stand up for yourself at any age, and for children, it's very difficult when they feel like they don't fit in. This book uses simple, engaging activities and methods drawn from child psychology to help your child grow their self-worth and feel comfortable in their own skin.

You may have noticed that your child seems to feel more self-conscious than other children, or is overly concerned with blending in with their peers. Sometimes it doesn't matter how much you remind them that they are wonderful just as they are—they just want to be like everybody else!

This book is aimed at children aged 8 to 12 years, a time of great changes and development in terms of their minds, bodies, academic and social lives— all of which can have an impact on their still-forming sense of self-worth. They'll experience exams for the first time, make close friendships, and, as their awareness of their bodies develops, they may begin to compare their attractiveness to that of others. It's also a time when some children get their first experiences with social media, puberty, and peer pressure. Children start to become aware with messages about which traits and body types are "desirable" and "undesirable." It's very understandable that some children might need help maintaining a healthy sense of self-worth during all these changes.

So, if you feel that your child may be suffering with low self-worth and is struggling to be themselves, rest assured that you're not alone and that you have the power to help them.

Signs of low self-worth

To help determine if your child has low self-worth, look out for these habits:

- They compare themselves to others (favorably or unfavorably)

- They are self-critical and hard on themselves

- They seem unsure of themselves and unable to make choices

- They are very concerned with fitting in

- They are strongly influenced by peer pressure

- They can become arrogant to disguise their feelings of low self-worth

- They seem reluctant to join in or take on new challenges

Try keeping a diary of when you notice these signs. It could be that there's a specific situation, place, or person that sends your child's self-worth plummeting. This way you can be better equipped to help your child.

The important thing to remember is: it's never too late to start helping your child feel comfortable being themselves.

Getting started

The way we as adults talk about ourselves has a huge effect on how our children see themselves. Like sponges, they absorb and learn how to think and talk about themselves from the things they observe in the adults in their families.

So, the best way to begin to talk about self-worth with your child is to talk about yourself kindly. Perhaps you could tell them something you're proud of, and relate it to something about themselves. Make a habit of praising things other than appearance—something your child has chosen or created themselves, an act of kindness or bravery . . . let them feel good about themselves for all kinds of reasons. Ask about the things they are interested in that are unfamiliar to you—let them be the expert and respect their taste and choices.

If there's something specific that's getting your child down, try gently helping them to think critically. Ask questions that challenge a negative world view—for example, "What if you're perfect just as you are?"

Building self-worth and a healthy sense of self is a habit rather than a quick transformation, so don't rush, panic, or criticize if you don't notice immediate effects. The benefits of learning how to be yourself will serve your child for a lifetime!

How to use this book

Introduce your child to this book and let them set the pace. They might like to read it with you or alone. Either way, see if you can get them talking about the things they learn and their thoughts and feelings about it.

The activities are designed to get children thinking about how they relate to themselves and the world around them, as well as encouraging creativity and celebrating differences. When your child feels secure in themselves, they are better equipped to deal with the challenges of everyday life. Let them know that you love and support them exactly as they are and that you trust them to know their own mind.

I hope this book helps your child feel free and comfortable to be themselves, enabling greater understanding of their own mind and the things that might knock their sense of self-worth. However, if you have serious worries about your child's self-image and mental health, your pediatrician is the best person to go to for further advice.

HOW TO USE THIS BOOK: A GUIDE FOR CHILDREN

These are signs that you may have low confidence:

♥ You feel shy or embarrassed about being yourself

♥ You find it hard to say what you really think and feel

♥ You feel like you aren't as good as other people

♥ You worry that you're very different from everyone else

If that sounds like you sometimes, or all of the time, you're not the only one. This book is for anyone who has a hard time being themselves. It's packed with activities and ideas that will help you feel more comfortable with yourself and raise your self-esteem.

You can read through the book and have a go at the activities at your own pace—there's no rush! There might be parts of the book that you'd like to talk through with an adult you trust and feel good talking to, and that's fine. This book is about you, so there are no wrong answers. You are the expert on you, and this book is here to help you see just how wonderful it is to be you, exactly as you are!

INTRODUCING GLOW THE MONSTER

Hi there, I'm Glow, and I'm excited to meet you! I'll help guide you through the activities and ideas in this book. Let's get cracking.

PART 1: WHAT IS SELF-WORTH?

Having a strong sense of self-worth means that you feel okay being yourself. It sounds simple, but it can be very hard for some of us! When you have high self-worth, it means you like yourself and know that you deserve good things, like fairness, being listened to, and being treated with kindness.

In this chapter, we'll learn more about self-worth and what makes you *you*.

How to spot low self-worth

You can't always easily tell when someone has low self-worth. Two people might act in very different ways because of low self-worth.

For some, it feels a lot easier and more comfortable to go along with the crowd—pretending to like, think, or be interested in certain things just because they are popular.

Some people might try to bully others into agreeing with their point of view—that's also a sign of low self-worth. When someone tries to control other people, it shows they aren't really sure that who they are is okay, so they try to change others so that they match.

Do you see how both ways of thinking and acting come from not being sure that it's okay to be different from others?

It takes a lot of bravery to show and be proud of the ways in which you're unique. Part of being yourself is also letting others be *them*selves and feeling okay with being different from one another.

ACTIVITY: ALL ABOUT ME

Can you complete the sentences so Glow can get to know you better? If you get stuck, it's okay to carry on to the next question.

My name is _____.

I am _____ years old.

My family is _____.

My friends are _____.

My hair is _____.

My body is _____.

My mind is _____.

My home is _____.

I feel happy when _____.

I feel upset when _____.

I feel angry when _____.

I feel worried about _____.

I feel good about _____.

I feel sad about _____.

My favorite thing to do is _____.

My least favorite thing to do is _____.

ACTIVITY: IF I WERE AN ANIMAL...

If you were an animal, what would you be? Write or draw about your animal self here!

I would be a _____

because _____.

I'd look like:

```
┌──────────────────────────────────────────┐
│                                            │
│                                            │
│                                            │
│                                            │
│                                            │
│                                            │
│                                            │
│                                            │
└──────────────────────────────────────────┘
```

♥ **Thinking about which animal you would choose to be and creating some art about it gives you the chance to reflect on your personality and how you see yourself.**

ACTIVITY: MY BEST BITS

What are the things you love most about yourself? Complete the sentences below—you can write as many things as you'd like!

I love that I can _____.

I love that I am _____.

I love that I have _____.

Signs of high and low self-worth

Having low self-worth feels like this:

- ♥ Disliking yourself

- ♥ Feeling that you are not as good as others

- ♥ Seeing the world as an unwelcoming place

- ♥ Speaking to yourself unkindly

- ♥ Not believing someone when they say something nice to or about you

- ♥ Feeling uncomfortable when you are on your own, or when you are with friends

- ♥ Looking on the worst side of everything

- ♥ Wanting desperately to fit in with others

- ♥ Wanting others to feel bad about their differences

- ♥ Feeling terrible when you make a small mistake

- ♥ Changing or lying about yourself to fit in

. . . and having high self-worth feels like this:

- ♥ Liking yourself

- ♥ Feeling that you're a good person

- ♥ Feeling confident

- ♥ Enjoying time both alone and with others

- ♥ Seeing the world as a friendly place

- ♥ Feeling happy when good things happen—big or small

- ♥ Encouraging others

- ♥ Respecting others' differences and your own

- ♥ Speaking to yourself kindly

- ♥ Accepting that you can make mistakes and learning from them

Feeling good about every bit of you

We all have things about ourselves that are easy to feel good about—perhaps for you it's your hair, your hobbies, how you are as a brother or sister . . . anything really! When we think about these things, or when someone else notices and comments on them, it usually makes us feel happy.

But everyone has things about themselves that they feel embarrassed or shy about—perhaps they even wish these things weren't true about them. Again, it could be anything—something about the way we look, think, feel, or act. When we think about these things, we might feel sad, and when someone notices them—even if they're not trying to be unkind—it can feel embarrassing or even hurtful.

Let's do some exploring in the activity on the next page. . . .

ACTIVITY: WHAT'S EASY TO FEEL GOOD ABOUT... AND WHAT'S HARD?

Can you write on the outline of the person below some things that you find easy to love about yourself—the types of things that make you feel happy to be yourself and that you like when people notice. (Remember, there are no wrong answers, but if you need some inspiration, how about: I'm funny, I'm clever, my bright eyes . . .)

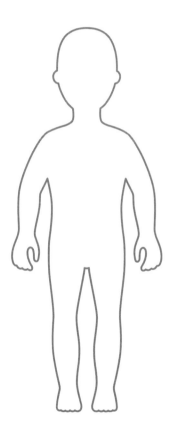

Now can you add one or two things to the shadow? Here, you can put the kind of thing that you might want to hide or change. You are the expert so you can write whatever comes into your mind.

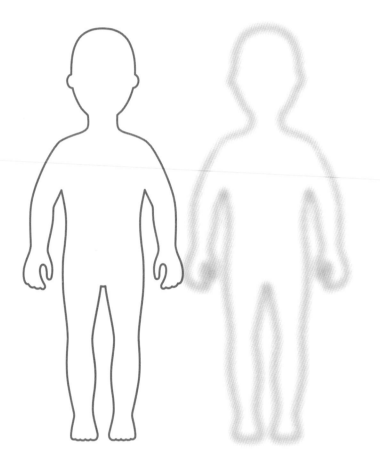

How does it feel to write these things down? It might be easy or hard, and that's okay. You're doing wonderfully.

ACTIVITY: BE MESSY

Right now, this page is pristine, blank, perfect . . . and so boring! Can you make it more interesting by messing it up a bit? Take a pencil, pen—or several pens —and scribble all over it.

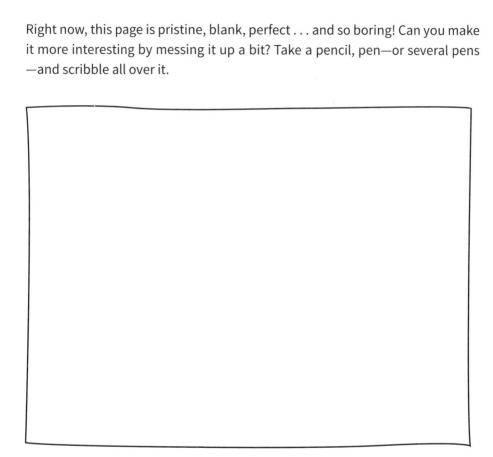

Amazing things can happen when you let yourself be messy and don't worry too much about how something's going to turn out. This is when you're at your most creative and your imagination is at its biggest. When you don't give too much attention to getting something perfect the first time, you're free to experiment and be yourself in whatever you do.

ACTIVITY: MY CAMOUFLAGE

Lots of animals use camouflage to make it harder for other animals to notice them. Some, like chameleons and octopuses, will even change the color of their skin to blend in to the background! Sometimes, everyone does things to help them fit in. For humans, it might mean dressing like everyone else, laughing at jokes that you don't find funny, or even telling people you're fine when you're not.

Color in the camouflage below whenever you feel like blending in to your surroundings.

I AM GROWING
AND LEARNING

PART 2: WHY IT'S GREAT TO BE UNIQUE

You may think there's a certain type of person that's "the best"—it might be someone you know in real life, a celebrity, or just an idea about how you "should" be.

The truth is, the world is home to seven billion unique human beings. Each one of us looks, thinks, feels, and acts in a way that's special to us. Also, each one of us has a different idea about what the "perfect" person might look like. While one person might dislike their curly hair and wish it were straight, a curly-haired person is just as likely to wish they had straight hair!

There is no one quite like you, and that's what makes you wonderful. In this chapter, we'll learn about ways of thinking that are more kind to ourselves and others.

ACTIVITY: WHEN DO I FEEL MY BEST... AND MY WORST?

Our sense of self-worth can go up and down depending on lots of other things. Who you're with, the things happening around you, how much energy you have, and what emotions you're feeling all contribute to your levels of self-worth.

It's important to remember that you deserve kindness and gentleness, even when you don't feel like you do. That is true of all human beings.

Are there people, places, or feelings that make you feel bad? Can you write them here?

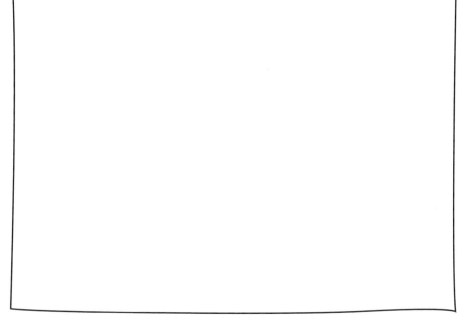

On this page, let's celebrate the people, places, and things that help you be truly yourself and feel good about it!

   Use the frames below to draw pictures or cut out and stick in photos:

What is self-talk?

Imagine if you had someone with you all the time, commenting on the things you do and say as well as how you look and feel. If that person was kind, gentle, and encouraging—like a best friend—how would that feel?

How about if that person was mean, rude, and bullying?

Self-talk is just like that person, except they're in our minds. It's the way we speak to and about ourselves, and if our self-talk voice is unkind, it's like having a bully with you all the time.

The good news is, you have the power to make your self-talk voice kinder—more like a best friend.

Can you think of any unkind thoughts you have about yourself? If you'd like, you can write them here:

_____

_____

_____

_____

Can you think of some kinder words you could say to yourself?

_____

_____

_____

_____

Thoughts are not real

Our brains are amazing things—they want to know absolutely everything! When there's something you're not sure about, your brain will make up a story to explain it.

For example, if you usually meet a particular friend between classes, but one day the friend doesn't show up, your brain might tell you one of these stories:

♥ They don't like me anymore

♥ Maybe they're off school today

♥ They're playing with other friends and leaving me out

♥ They must be running late—I'll wait a bit longer

Now, these stories can't *all* be true! The story your brain makes up usually has more to do with how you feel about yourself than what has actually happened. Can you choose one of the kinder stories?

It's okay if your brain makes up negative stories. Try telling yourself that the stories might not be true. Then try choosing a story that's more positive. Look for facts to prove the negative story wrong—for example, something kind your friend said to you yesterday, how long you've been friends, that you haven't done anything to upset them.

This might feel uncomfortable or silly at first—but the more you practice, the easier it gets!

Quieting unkind thoughts

Sometimes our unkind thoughts can get really loud, and it's hard to ignore them when they do. If you can recognize when you're being unkind to yourself, that's the biggest and most important step toward growing your self-worth!

What can you do when you're struggling with unkind thoughts?

I can...

♥ *Say or write a positive message to myself*

♥ *Wrap myself in a soft blanket*

♥ *Have a drink of water*

♥ *Have a snack*

♥ *Take a break*

♥ *Go outside*

♥ *Do something nice for a friend or family member*

♥ *Do some drawing or coloring*

♥ *Move my body*

♥ *Play a brain-based game (like Sudoku or a crossword)*

♥ *Do some breathing exercises (see opposite page)*

_____

_____

_____

ACTIVITY: TAKE DEEP BREATHS

Taking a deep breath helps quiet your mind and calm your body.

Try finger breathing when you're having trouble with thoughts or feelings of any kind. Here's how:

Hold out one hand and slowly trace the index finger of your other hand from the base of your thumb, up and over, down between your thumb and finger, up and down. As you trace upward, breathe in. As you trace downward, breathe out. Keep going for as long as you need to.

You can also finger breathe by drawing around your hand. When you draw up your finger, breathe in, and when you draw down, breathe out. Try it here.

ACTIVITY: A TIME I WAS BRAVE

Can you think of a time you were brave? Bravery isn't just about fighting a tiger or climbing a really tall tree—although those things can be brave, too! True bravery is when something (and it could be literally anything, from taking part in a race to admitting you've made a mistake) feels scary to you, but you do it because it's the right thing to do.

One of the bravest things you can do is to share your feelings. In fact, that's often the first step of a brave act. Saying "this scares me" lets those around you know what's difficult for you.

Use the space here to write about a time you were brave:

_____

_____

_____

_____

I LIKE
MYSELF

ACTIVITY: BEING THANKFUL

When you take a little time every day to feel grateful, it helps you accept yourself exactly as you are and appreciate all the good things in your life right at this moment.

Can you write something you're grateful for, starting with each letter of the alphabet? It could be anything, big or small! A memory, a toy, a person, a place, a tree . . .

A _____   N _____

B _____   O _____

C _____   P _____

D _____   Q _____

E _____   R _____

F _____   S _____

G _____   T _____

H _____   U _____

I _____   V _____

J _____   W _____

K _____   X _____

L _____   Y _____

M _____   Z _____

One-minute visualization

When you want to relax, try a one-minute visualization like this one. Try reading this yourself, or ask someone else to read it to you in a calm, gentle voice, then set a timer and picture yourself as a tortoise:

Imagine you are a tortoise. Feel your sturdy feet on the ground, the strong shell on your back. You go at your own pace and you carry your home with you wherever you go. Your body is a home to you and you are safe.

You stop for a while in a grassy meadow. You can hear a gentle breeze rustling through the tall grass and the wildflowers. You look up to the sky; it's bright blue, with a few fluffy white clouds drifting slowly across it. You can smell the fresh air all around you.

You're ready for a nap, so you snuggle into your shell. What's it like inside? Are there patterns on the walls? It fits you perfectly, and you feel safe and content here. Stay here as long as you'd like, and when you're ready, you can stretch your arms, legs, and head out of your shell. Now you can open your eyes, take a deep breath, and go back to your day.

ACTIVITY: HELP GLOW FEEL BETTER!

Just like you, Glow is wonderfully unique! Glow's thoughts, feelings, likes and dislikes, the way Glow looks, and the choices Glow makes all work together to make Glow a one-of-a-kind monster.

But just like everyone, there are things that Glow feels shy about.

What could you say to help Glow accept these things? Write some kind words that will help Glow feel better in the bubbles…

For this exercise, you might like to think back to the things you wrote in the shadow on page 24. These are the things that you're shy about, things that make you feel like the odd one out.

> ♥ **The truth is, a lot of us are very hard on ourselves. If you can accept and be kind to the parts of yourself that you find tricky to like, in time they will feel easier and easier to deal with.**

ACTIVITY: POSITIVE-THOUGHT BRACELETS

Wearing something that reminds you of positive thoughts can really help when you have a tricky moment. It can be hard to find courage and remember to be yourself *all* the time, whether you're chatting to your friends, talking to an adult, or just going about your day.

Using the instructions below, you could make a bracelet, key chain, or bag charm to help you feel strong and confident all day long.

You will need:

♥   Mixed beads

♥   Elastic cord

Instructions:

Take a good look at your selection of beads. Notice their colors and textures. Can you match them up with positive thoughts? For example, a blue bead could match with the positive thought "I am calm" and a heart-shaped bead might be "I am loved." You can use your imagination and the matches don't have to make sense to anyone but you!

Once you've matched some beads to some positive thoughts, thread them on to the elastic. You can make a pattern and use the same color beads more than once—whatever feels right. When your bracelet is the right length, tie the ends of the elastic close to the beads with a double knot and thread the elastic ends back through the beads closest to the knot.

Now, whenever you wear your bracelet, you'll be reminded of the positive thoughts that go with the beads. Look at or think of your bracelet every time you're bothered by negative thoughts. Write down some of your positive thoughts in the spaces below.

_____

_____

_____

_____

_____

_____

_____

_____

Everyone is different, inside and out!

People come in different shapes, sizes, and colors. We all like different things, think different things, and make different choices.

Messages about how you "should" feel and what you "should" like come to us every day—from TV, books, people around us, advertisements, and the internet. You've probably heard things about how boys and girls are supposed to think, act, and feel. We get so many of these messages that it can feel like they are true.

The truth is, you don't have to believe these things! Just because you are a boy doesn't mean you have to like "boy things"; just because you are a girl doesn't mean you have to like "girl things." You can like "you things."

ACTIVITY: COMPARING YOURSELF TO OTHERS

Sometimes you might find yourself comparing yourself to other kids your age or older. What kind of things do you admire in others that make you feel like you want to be more like them? Write them here:

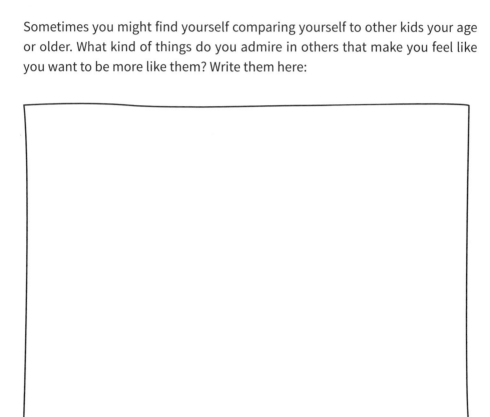

It's very natural to compare yourself to others—everyone does it . . . even the ones who seem perfect! It becomes a problem when it makes you feel bad, makes you want to change things about yourself, or makes you want to be unkind to other people.

Can you think of something about yourself that others might admire? Use this space to write as many things as you'd like!

We all have different strengths . . . and different worries about ourselves! Try to remember that you are just amazing exactly as you are, and you don't need to change anything about yourself.

Love your body

Your body is incredible! Every single part of your body is just right for you. Your body works hard every day to keep you breathing, laughing, learning, and playing.

Kids your age grow an average of 2.36 inches (6 centimeters) every year, and you'll see your body change in other ways when puberty starts. These changes might make you feel confused, worried, or embarrassed, and these feelings are perfectly normal. Everyone experiences these changes, and you can always talk to a trusted friend or adult about anything that's troubling you.

At every age, your body belongs to you. No one is allowed to see or touch your body if you don't want them to.

Every body is beautiful

You might have a picture in your mind of which types of body are "good" and which are "bad." Your body is beautiful just as it is, and there is no need for you to listen to anyone else telling you your body should be bigger or smaller, taller or shorter . . . or different in any way. Our bodies are as unique as our personalities, and guess what? Your body is just right for you, and you don't exist for other people to look at!

Care for your body—feed it healthy food, move it around in ways that make you feel happy and alive. Listen to your body and you will hear it tell you when something's uncomfortable, hurtful, or simply not right for you.

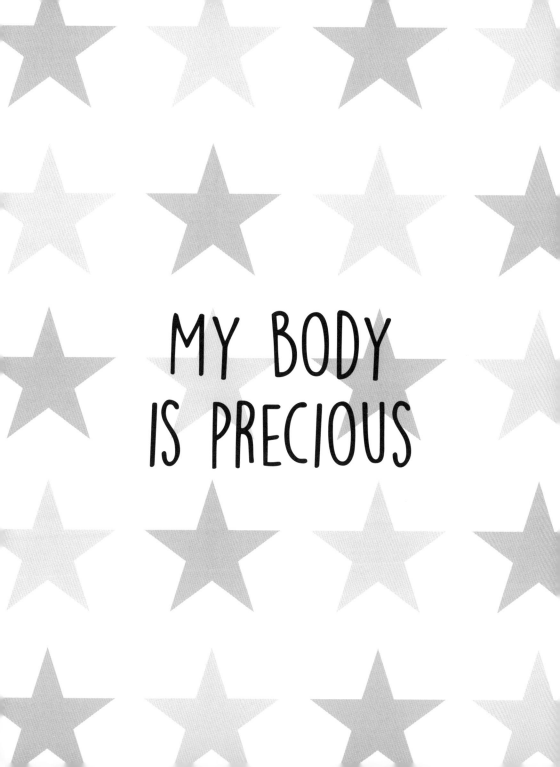

PART 3:
IN THEIR SHOES

We've talked a lot about the ways in which everyone is different . . . but we are also very similar in many ways. Deep down, everyone wants to be treated with kindness—we just show it in different ways.

It can be tricky sometimes to remember other people's feelings, especially when we have our own feelings to think about!

In this chapter, we'll learn about being yourself while at the same time letting others be themselves.

ACTIVITY: WHAT IS EMPATHY?

Empathy means being able to understand how someone else is feeling, and to imagine how you would feel in their situation. Often you can tell how someone is feeling from looking at them but not always. Some people are very good at hiding how they feel!

Let's try out a bit of empathy with Glow. Below are some things that have happened to Glow. Try to imagine how Glow might feel. Write the emotion or emotions Glow might be feeling underneath each situation.

Glow answers a question correctly in class.

_____

Glow's pet is ill and has to visit the vet.

_____

Glow is walking home and it starts to rain.

_____

Glow is having a birthday party today.

_____

Glow's friend borrowed Glow's favorite game and broke it.

_____

Glow is going on vacation next week.

_____

> ♥ We're all quite similar when it comes to emotions, so if you can imagine how you would feel, that's probably pretty close to how another person feels.

We are all patchworks!

Patchwork means lots of different pieces of fabric sewn together to make a beautiful, colorful blanket. While in many ways we're all very similar, at the same time, our feelings, the way we act, and the choices we make can be very different! That's because our personalities are made up of all the things we've seen, heard, and done in our lives—just like a patchwork.

Glow thinks it's very important to follow the rules of a game, and it upsets Glow when the rules aren't followed properly (perhaps because a game was once ruined when the rules weren't followed, or because Glow's family talked a lot about following rules).

For Glow's friend Fiz, the rules aren't that important and Fiz gets upset when someone tries to make them follow the rules (maybe Fiz hasn't played many games with rules before, or Fiz's family is more interested in being creative than in following rules).

It can be hard to get along when our personalities clash in this kind of way! Neither monster is right or wrong—they just see things differently.

If we knew all of each other's memories and experiences, the different ways we behave would make perfect sense to us all. But it's not possible to know very many people that well! So it's best to always be kind to yourself and others, and if someone behaves in a way that hurts or upsets you, know that it's not your fault. We are all patchworks, after all.

ACTIVITY: FAVORITE THINGS GAME

We've learned a lot about thinking of others and appreciating our differences so far in this book. Here's a game you can play with a friend or someone in your family:

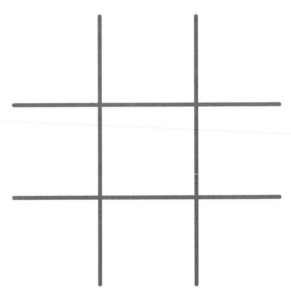

> ♥ **How to play: For two players. Each pick a different color pen or pencil. Take turns to write one of your favorite things in each square (you could write your favorite food, color, animal... anything you can think of!). The winner is the first person to get three in a row of their favorite things.**

This game will help you learn about each other as well as have fun!

ACTIVITY: WHEN SOMEONE ELSE IS FEELING DIFFICULT EMOTIONS

How does it feel when someone close to you is feeling a tricky emotion, like anger or sadness? Circle the feelings and sensations you feel.

Panic

I want to hide

Headache

Crying

Relaxed

I want to run away

My heart hurts

I want to make them happy

I think it's funny

We can feel all kinds of things around other people, especially when one of us is feeling big emotions! Sometimes they're like germs, and we can start to feel the same emotions as the other person. Sometimes we want to comfort them and sometimes we want to move away. All of those feelings are okay!

ACTIVITY: WHEN YOU NEED TO SAY SORRY

Sometimes we hurt our friends' feelings by accident, or even on purpose. When people spend time together, there will always be times when we disagree, want our own way, or feel big emotions.

When you've hurt someone unfairly—perhaps by calling them names, trying to make them feel bad about themselves, hitting or pushing them—you need to make it right.

It takes a lot of courage to say sorry and admit when you've made a mistake. Try taking three deep breaths (this helps calm down your mind and body so you can think more clearly) and be kind to yourself. You are a human being—we all make mistakes! You are not a bad person just because you got something wrong. The most important thing is how you make things right.

If you follow these steps when you say sorry, you'll look after your own feelings as well as the other person's:

I'm sorry for _____.

It was wrong because _____.

Next time I'll _____.

How can I make it better? _____.

On this page, can you write or draw about a time you needed to say sorry? How did it feel? What did you do? Would you act differently next time?

ACTIVITY: WHEN SOMEONE HAS HURT YOU

When your feelings or body have been hurt, it can be difficult to let it show. Sometimes, it feels easier and more comfortable to act as if you aren't bothered . . . as if your feelings don't matter.

Your feelings and your body *do* matter, and if someone has hurt you—on purpose or by accident—you are allowed to say so and you are allowed to get away from them. It might not always feel comfortable or safe to say these things to the person who has hurt you, so if that's the case, you can go to a trusted friend or adult.

Here are some words you could use if this is tricky for you:

That's not fair.

That hurts.

That makes me feel _____.

Ouch!

Stop – I don't like that.

I'm going to walk away now and tell my parents.

Can you think of a time someone hurt your body or your feelings? What happened? What did you say? What would you like to have said? Write or draw about it below.

ACTIVITY: PRACTICE PAUSING

Sometimes, friends might hurt each other and it's not clear who's right and who's wrong. . . . Sometimes no one's in the wrong!

You can always do your best to look after your feelings as well as others' but sometimes it can be hard to see how to solve a problem—especially if you're feeling big emotions yourself!

When someone's feelings are hurt by something you've said or done, it doesn't always mean you're in the wrong. When everyone's feeling big emotions, it helps to press pause on things for a moment.

Here are some ways to press pause to help cool down an argument:

♥   Take three deep breaths

♥   Count to ten

♥   Step away and look out of the window

♥   Spot three blue things in the space around you

Pausing helps calm your body and mind so you can think more clearly. If you can get everyone to join in, that'd be so much better! Once you're feeling calmer, try looking for solutions to the problem rather than working out who is to blame.

For example, your friend might be upset that it's your turn in a game that they want to play.

Instead of ignoring them, press pause and ask yourself what you could do to resolve the situation. Write or draw your ideas here:

Ways to feel calmer
••

Our minds, bodies, and emotions are all linked. When human beings feel big
emotions, we feel them all over!

Big and difficult emotions like fear, panic, anger, and sadness can feel like a
big wave crashing over you. When your body feels this way, it means your brain
senses danger and your nervous system is working really hard to keep you safe.

> ♥ **Your nervous system is made up of your brain, your spine, and the**
> **nerves that reach to every part of your body. It's how the different**
> **parts of your body get messages to and from your brain, including**
> **everything you see, smell, touch, taste, and hear.**

This happens because our brains are hardwired to keep us safe from danger. To
our brains, anything that makes us feel big, difficult emotions is a threat—even
if it can't really hurt us.

There are lots of ways to calm down if you're feeling this way. Scientists have discovered that rhythmic, repetitive activities help calm the brainstem, which connects your brain to the rest of your body, including your nervous system.

Here are some brainstem calmers to try:

♥   Playing catch

♥   Drumming

♥   Bouncing on a trampoline

♥   Breathing exercises (see page 35)

♥   Walking/marching

♥   Stroking an animal

♥   Singing

ACTIVITY: MY FAVORITE THINGS

What are your favorite things? The things you like are unique, and you don't have to like the same things as everyone else!

Sometimes it might feel like there are things you "should" like or enjoy, because a lot of other people your age like them, or there are commercials on TV or the internet that make them look cool. Part of being yourself is having your own opinions and favorites.

It's okay to like some of the same things as others your age, and it's okay to like different things, too! Let yourself like what *you* like.

My favorite song is...

_____

_____

My favorite color is...

_____

_____

My favorite outfit is...

_____

_____

My favorite book is...

_____

_____

My favorite TV show is...

_____

_____

My favorite game is...

_____

_____

Something a lot of my friends like but I don't is...

_____

_____

ACTIVITY: TRY NEW THINGS

Being a beginner can be really hard. Glow has just joined a rock-climbing club. Everyone else is so good at it! Glow feels embarrassed and wants to quit.

The thing that Glow is forgetting is that everyone is a bit terrible when they're just starting to learn. From walking and talking to reading and writing, riding a bike to using a computer . . . we were all beginners once!

Can you remember your first time doing something that you're now really good at? Here's a challenge that will show you the power of practicing: Can you write your name backwards? Try it—it's really hard!

But, if you keep practicing, you'll notice it becomes easier and easier. Keep writing your name backwards here.

Can you see yourself getting quicker at it and your writing becoming neater? With practice, you can master almost any new skill!

ACTIVITY: THE HERO OF YOUR OWN STORY

Everyone is the center of their own universe and the hero of the story of their life. No two people see the world in the same way because we can only truly see it through our own eyes, with our own patchwork of memories and experiences.

Each thing that happens is felt in a unique way by each person it happens to. We notice different things, feel different emotions, and think different thoughts.

It's Glow's birthday party! Glow's friends Pip and Bop have given Glow the same present.

Can you try telling the story from two points of view?

First, try telling the story as if you were Glow. What would Glow notice? What feelings would Glow have? What kind of thoughts?

_____

_____

_____

_____

_____

_____

_____

_____

_____

Now, have a go at telling the same story, but this time write as if you were Bop. Imagine the kind of things Bop would notice at the party. What feelings and thoughts would Bop have?

_____

_____

_____

_____

_____

_____

_____

_____

The two stories you wrote are probably quite different in some ways, even though they're about the same thing!

PART 4:
EXPRESS YOURSELF

You are allowed to be yourself. Even if other people find you unusual or hard to understand, that doesn't mean you're doing something wrong.

Letting your true self shine might mean some people don't like you. That's okay. You're not for everyone and not everyone is a good fit to be your friend. Those people will find their own friends by being themselves!

In this chapter, we'll look at ways to let your true self shine.

Celebrate everyone's uniqueness!

Perhaps there's something about the way you look, the way you act, the things you are interested in, or the way you think that's quite unusual.

You should never be made to feel bad because you are different.

Some people find it hard to respect those who are different from them—it might be your skin color, language, a medical condition, the way your mind works, or your opinions. If someone has a problem with any of these things, it is not your problem to solve. You are brilliant and perfect just as you are.

Examples of disrespect might be name-calling, leaving you out, not sharing with you, or ignoring you.

We should all respect each other *and* ourselves. So, if someone's not showing you respect, you can walk away from them.

ACTIVITY: MAKE A SMILE GUIDE

We all like our families and friends to show us how much they love us, but different things feel more or less comfortable for different people. Some of us like having our hair stroked; others appreciate a thoughtful gift or encouraging words.

Can you make a smile guide for your loved ones?

Think about how you like to be treated when you're sad, tired, or sick . . . and how you like to have fun when you're feeling great.

Here are some examples to get you started:

I like it when Mom puts a blanket over me while I'm watching TV.

I like singing along to music using silly voices.

When I hear encouraging words, I feel fantastic.

_____

_____

_____

_____

_____

_____

Create your smile guide on this page (or on a separate piece of paper). You could use words, pictures, collage, symbols . . . whatever you like!

♥ Once you've finished, show your smile guide to your friends and family—they might even like to make their own!

ACTIVITY: MAKE A SELF-PORTRAIT

Can you draw yourself on the next page? Remember: your portrait doesn't need to be perfect, neat, or realistic, and there is no "good" or "bad" way to be creative. You can use pencils, pens, pastels, paint, collage . . . anything you like!

> ♥ **Extra challenge: can you draw yourself as if your feelings and thoughts can be seen from the outside? They might be tattoos, colors, patterns . . .**

Create your self-portrait here!

ACTIVITY: YOUR FRIENDS

Do you have a best friend or more than one good friend? What do you have in common with your friends? Perhaps you have the same hair color, favorite sport, least favorite subject . . . Write or draw about the things you share here:

Can you think of the ways in which you and your friends are different from each other? Write or draw about them here:

ACTIVITY: HOW TO SAY HARD THINGS WITH KINDNESS

Sometimes your friends might ask for your opinion—perhaps they'd like to know what you think about a painting they've made or their new hairstyle. What happens if you don't like it?

It's tempting to lie in a situation like this, especially if you might hurt your friend's feelings.

A good way of saying something tricky to a friend is to make a sandwich out of it and say something tricky (the filling) in the middle of two nice things (the bread). Try the example below.

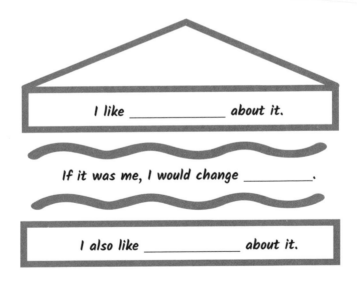

I like _____ about it.

If it was me, I would change _____.

I also like _____ about it.

That way, you've stayed true to yourself and said what you really think, while still being gentle with your friend's feelings.

Can you think of a time you had something tricky like that to say to a friend?
Could you try making a sandwich of your own?

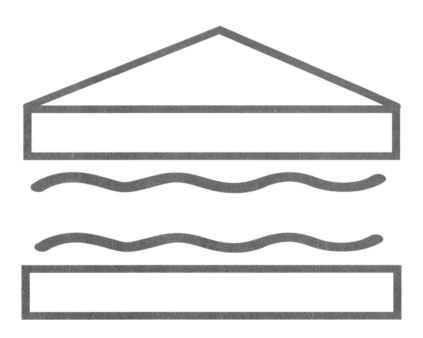

ACTIVITY: DRAW YOUR BREATH

Imagine your breath changed color depending on how you were feeling. What color would happiness be? How about fear or confusion?

Glow is feeling nervous and excited. Although to the human eye monsters' breath is invisible, in monster land it is colorful. For example, when Glow is feeling nervous and excited, Glow's breath is green, purple, and orange.

Can you draw your own colorful breath picture? Use as many or as few colors as you like. You could even hold your picture up to your face and exhale, imagining your breath in many colors.

ACTIVITY: HOW DO I SHOW MY EMOTIONS?

What do you do on the outside when you're feeling big emotions? How do they feel on the inside? You can do this activity all at once, or come back to it during or after you feel each emotion.

   You can write, draw, scribble . . . use color, poetry . . . whatever best describes your emotions is great.

For example:
When I'm angry . . .
On the inside I feel like a swirling whirlpool.
On the outside I frown and I raise my voice.

When I'm worried...

On the inside _____.

On the outside _____.

When I'm happy...

On the inside _____.

On the outside _____.

When I'm sad...

On the inside _____.

On the outside _____.

When I'm excited...

On the inside _____.

On the outside _____.

When I'm bored...

On the inside _____.

On the outside _____.

ACTIVITY: SAYING NO

It can be hard to say no sometimes, especially if we think we might hurt someone's feelings. Sometimes, we even hurt our own feelings by saying yes when we'd really, really like to say no.

A lot of the time, saying no takes courage. Practicing ways to say no with some added kindness can help you feel braver.

If you say no with kindness and the other person still tries to change it into a yes, you don't have to go along with it. Stick to your no and say something like "Stop—I don't like that." You can take the kindness out: the word no is enough on its own! If someone is hurting you, or doing something that makes you feel uncomfortable or afraid, you can say no really firmly.

ACTIVITY: KEEP A MOOD TRACKER

Keeping a record of how you feel each day helps form a habit of tuning in to your emotions.

   Asking yourself "How am I feeling?" helps you stay true to yourself and learn more about your ups and downs.

   Create a key—perhaps a color or symbol for each emotion or mood.

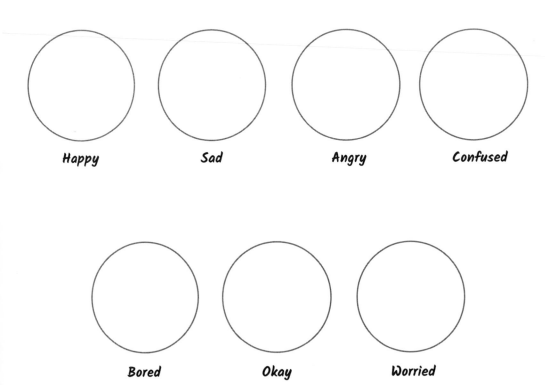

Happy   **Sad**   **Angry**   **Confused**

Bored   **Okay**   **Worried**

Every day, fill in one square to show how you felt in general that day. You might start to notice patterns!

	Jan	Feb	Mar	Apr	May	Jun	Jul	Aug	Sep	Oct	Nov	Dec
1												
2												
3												
4												
5												
6												
7												
8												
9												
10												
11												
12												
13												
14												
15												
16												
17												
18												
19												
20												
21												
22												
23												
24												
25												
26												
27												
28												
29												
30												
31												

ACTIVITY: EMOJI EMOTIONS

If you find it hard to talk about your feelings, why not use emojis? You could use the emojis below and on the next page to start a conversation with a parent, caregiver, friend, or teacher.

> ♥ **Emojis were invented to express emotions in text messages.**

Using emojis might be easier than talking out loud about how you feel inside, especially if you're feeling big, difficult, and complicated emotions.

Happy	Sad	Peaceful

Annoyed	Fed up	Playful

These are just a few, and they might not be just right for how you're feeling. Can you invent some of your own emojis to show how you're feeling right now?

WE ARE
ALL UNIQUE

PART 5: TAKING CARE OF YOURSELF

When you take time to look after your body, mind, and emotions, you're showing yourself love. People with high self-worth make sure that their bodies and minds have everything they need so that they can get on with being themselves and enjoying life!

In this chapter, we'll explore all the ways you can care for yourself.

Healthy eating

Eating a good, balanced diet will keep your body healthy, help you feel your best, and give you plenty of energy. What's more, when you eat well, it's much easier to regulate your emotions and speak kindly to yourself.

So, what is a healthy diet? A healthy diet means a balanced diet—so you can still have your favorite treats and be healthy, as long as you balance them out with plenty of:

Fruit

Vegetables

Whole grains (like whole-wheat bread, oats, and brown rice)

Protein (like eggs, fish, and tofu)

Healthy oils (like olive or coconut oil)

ACTIVITY: DRINK PLENTY OF WATER

Our bodies are made up of more than 60 percent water, and we lose some of it every time we breathe out, sweat, cry, or go to the bathroom.

Kids need to drink at least six to eight glasses of water per day to stay healthy and hydrated. When you have enough water in your body, it's easier to feel calm, concentrate, use your memory, and have fun.

Challenge yourself to drink eight glasses of water every day this week!

So you can keep track, color in one of the water drops here every time you drink a glass of water.

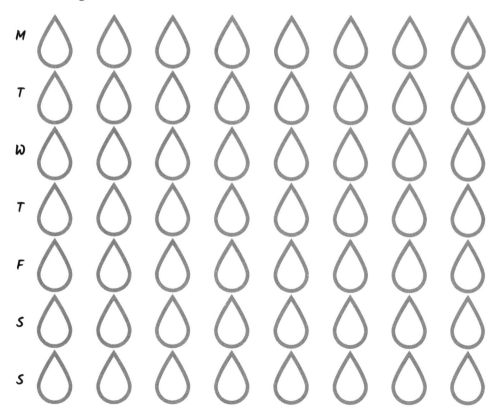

Be careful when cutting out this page

A good night's sleep

Getting enough sleep will help you wake up feeling good about the day and good about yourself! It's tempting to stay up late reading, playing, or thinking, but getting plenty of sleep will mean your brain is better prepared to do those things in the daytime.

When we sleep, it gives our minds a chance to make sense of the things that have happened or been on our minds. Often, problems that are bugging you at bedtime can feel a lot more manageable after a good night's sleep.

Do you ever have trouble falling asleep? Try this breathing exercise to help you relax:

Close your eyes and breathe in through your nose to the count of five, imagining your breath filling your whole body from the top of your head to the tips of your toes.

Now breathe out through your mouth to the count of seven, imagining the breath drifting slowly out of your mouth and up into the night sky.

Keep going, concentrating on your breath all the time . . . until you fall asleep.

Emotional needs

What are emotional needs? They are the things we need to feel in order to feel safe and okay being ourselves—and we sometimes need the people around us to help us feel these emotions.

All human beings need to feel:

♥ Safe

♥ Loved

♥ Understood

♥ Accepted

When we don't feel these things, it's extremely hard to feel okay to be ourselves. Just like we need to sleep, eat, drink, and exercise, we also need to feel good, calm, and safe with the people we spend most of our time with. Our family members, teachers, and friends will all affect our emotions.

There are all sorts of things we do—sometimes without thinking—to help us feel safe and okay. For example . . .

♥ Ask for a hug or a chat

♥ Do something noisy to get your parents' attention

♥ Do something nice for your parent or caregiver

♥ Check with an adult to make sure you're safe

It's okay to ask for attention, love, and reassurance from those around you.

ACTIVITY: BE YOUR OWN BEST FRIEND

Remember that you deserve to be treated kindly. There is no one in the world who is allowed to treat you badly—including yourself!

Talk to and treat yourself like you would your best friend. That means seeing the best in you, doing things you enjoy, and talking about the good and bad things in your life.

What kind of things do best friends say to each other and do for each other? Can you write down some ideas here?

For example: listen to you, say nice things, share their sweets.

What best friends say and do

Get plenty of exercise

Keeping active—which could be anything from walking to dancing, playing sports to climbing trees—helps keep your body feeling good. What you might not realize is that it also helps your mind feel good, too!

When we exercise, our brains release special chemicals that make us feel better all over. Exercise is also a brilliant way to stop upsetting thoughts from going round in your head—when you're concentrating on your body, you can take a break from those kinds of thoughts.

Try to be active for an hour or more each day doing something you enjoy!

I AM IMPORTANT

ACTIVITY: HOW ARE YOU DOING?

It's time to check in with yourself. What are you finding difficult right now?
What makes you feel sad, worried, or scared?

What's going well in your life right now?

ACTIVITY: ASKING FOR HELP

Glow is stuck on a math problem, but everyone else in Glow's class seems to be finding their work easy! Glow feels very shy about asking for help.

What might Glow be thinking?

What would you say to Glow to help Glow feel braver about asking for help?

♥ Asking for help when you feel like you're the only one who needs it can be really scary! Try to remember what we learned on page 32: thoughts are not real. You are allowed to ask for help with anything you find tricky, even if it doesn't look like anyone else finds it tricky at all. Some of them probably do but aren't brave enough to say so!

ACTIVITY: RELAX WITH COLORING

You deserve some downtime! Why not chill out and do some coloring?

ACTIVITY: WHAT DO YOU FIND RELAXING?

Taking time to relax is an important part of keeping your mind and body happy and healthy. Why not try one of these chilled-out activities?

- ♥ Do some stretches (see page 121)

- ♥ Write a poem

- ♥ Read a book

- ♥ Choose an object to draw

- ♥ Go for a bike ride

- ♥ Play with slime or modelling clay

Look for positives

It can sometimes be hard, when you're feeling unhappy, to see all the good things in your life. When you feel this way, it's okay. You don't have to be happy all the time.

When you're ready to start feeling a bit happier, it can help to find one small, good thing.

Can you start a list here of some small, good things that you could come back to when you're feeling down?

It could be the words of a song, a smell, a pen that feels really cool to write with . . .

_____

_____

_____

_____

_____

_____

_____

I CAN ASK
FOR HELP

PART 6:
SELF-ACCEPTANCE

We've come to the final part of the book—well done! This chapter is all about self-acceptance. That means feeling okay with yourself exactly as you are. When you accept yourself, you know that you can trust yourself to make good choices, be brave when you need to, and be kind to yourself always.

ACTIVITY: THE FUTURE IS TODAY

What's one thing you'll do later on today? (Or tomorrow, if you're reading this at bedtime!) It might be a piece of work, a game with friends, or part of your everyday routine. Perhaps you could choose something that you find tricky or you're worried about.

Can you picture yourself doing it? Close your eyes and imagine you are there right now—you don't need to be different in any way, just yourself. Now imagine it going really well.

Can you draw a quick sketch or write a few sentences about it?

♥ **Try visualizing your future self each morning. It can help influence how your day goes!**

ACTIVITY: FIND YOUR HAPPY PLACE

Can you think of a place—real, from your imagination, or a mix of both—where you feel happy, safe, and relaxed? A place where you can be yourself completely.

Take some time to draw and write about this place. The more detail you give it, the more real it will feel. Then when you need to be calm, relaxed, and confident, you can picture yourself in this happy place.

Write about your happy place here. Try using all of your senses.

What can you see?

_____

_____

What can you hear?

_____

_____

What can you smell?

_____

_____

What can you feel?

_____

_____

What can you taste?

_____

_____

Draw your happy place on this page. You could draw a map, a self-portrait, a landscape . . . whatever feels right!

ACTIVITY: SHAPE STRETCHES

Stretching helps relax your body and your mind. Can you make your body into these shapes? See if you can hold the stretch while you count from one to twenty.

Square: start on your hands and knees, like a square.

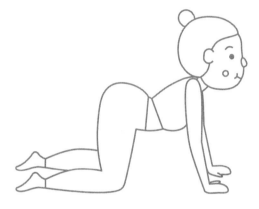

Triangle: now straighten your legs and put your feet flat on the ground to make a triangle.

Rectangle: put your hands and your toes on the ground, making your body a straight line between them.

Circle: now curl yourself into a circle by tucking your knees under your chin, resting your forehead on the ground, and extending your arms behind you.

ACTIVITY: SELF-TALK SWITCHES

How do you talk to and about yourself? Perhaps it's changed since you started reading this book, or perhaps it's about the same.

One thing you can do if you're talking unkindly to or about yourself is to switch the words you use. Take an unkind phrase and change it a bit to make it kinder.

Unkind thoughts	Make it kinder
Example: I'm stupid.	Example: I'm trying my best.

I LOVE BEING ME

Unkind thoughts	Make it kinder

ACTIVITY: HOW WOULD MY FRIENDS DESCRIBE ME?

What words would your friends use to describe you? You can guess them yourself or ask your besties to fill in this page and the next one!

ACTIVITY: COLLECT BE-YOURSELF BOOSTS!

Write some self-worth boosters on the opposite page—you can cut them out and keep them in a jar or a scrapbook to look at when you're feeling down. (Remember to take care when using scissors.)

Collect compliments, quotes, achievements, happy moments—and anything else that makes you feel good—for when you need a little boost.

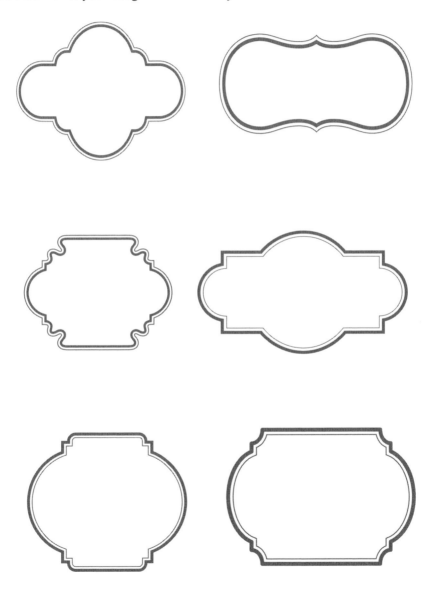

Be careful when cutting out this page

ACTIVITY: KEEP WRITING!

Just because you're getting to the end of the activities in this book doesn't mean you should stop writing about yourself, the things you love, and the things you find tricky. Why not start a diary, or keep a notebook handy for whenever you'd like to put some of your thoughts into writing.

An easy way to write about your day is to think of one thing that was good, one thing that was hard, and one thing that was okay. Try it on the next page!

One thing that was good today...

_____

_____

One thing that was hard today...

_____

_____

One thing that was okay today...

_____

_____

What have you learned so far?

In this book, we've talked about:

- ♥ How special and unique you are.

- ♥ That it's okay to express your true feelings.

- ♥ That you don't need to change anything about yourself in order to deserve kindness and respect.

- ♥ That every human being on the planet is special and unique, and that at the same time, we have lots and lots in common with one another.

- ♥ That your body and mind are precious and taking good care of them is an important job, so in Part 5 we looked at all the ways we can look after ourselves.

- ♥ That it's important to be clear in how you like to be treated and to ask for what you need, so we learned about that, too!

What was the most interesting or surprising thing you've learned in this book?

_____

_____

_____

_____

ACTIVITY: LOVE YOURSELF ACTION PLAN

What can I do when I feel down, upset, or embarrassed about myself? I can . . .

♥ Take a deep breath

♥ Talk to someone I trust

♥ Play

♥ Draw

♥ Go outside

♥ Feel my feelings

♥ Talk to myself kindly

♥ Write it down

_____

_____

_____

_____

The end

Glow's had a wonderful time learning all about self-worth and being yourself—have you enjoyed it, too? Remember: you can come back to this book any time you like—whether you're looking for a self-worth-boosting activity or want to explain the idea of self-worth to a friend.

You've done really well and should be super proud of yourself! Don't forget to let yourself shine, and always be yourself!

For parents: How to help your child be themselves

Being yourself is a tricky and hard-to-define thing. We all change, grow, and evolve throughout our lives, and children do so at a much faster rate than adults! We can marvel at the ability of our children to adapt and build resilience, but sometimes staying true to themselves means dealing with difficult emotions and thoughts, as well as treasuring and enjoying their uniqueness.

The best thing you can do to help your child cultivate a healthy sense of self-worth is to model one yourself. Talk to yourself and others with kindness and compassion. Honor and celebrate your differences, as well as what you have in common with others. Be yourself and talk about your emotions, opinions, and tastes in an open way that allows your child to share their own.

Talk about your life outside of being a parent! Showing your child that you're a whole and complicated human being, just like everyone else, will help them appreciate their own complexities.

When something goes wrong, a mistake is made, or there's an argument or conflict, try to focus on the problem rather than blaming someone or working out how it could have been avoided. Look at the situation carefully and work out how to make it right.

Help your child accept the difficult emotions that are part of life by validating and sitting with those emotions, rather than minimizing them or trying to talk your child out of sadness or fear. If your child learns that they can feel these feelings and be okay, it will help them grow into confident, intuitive adults with integrity.

Talk to your child about diversity and teach them how to show respect to others, as well as themselves. If your child can appreciate differences in the people they meet, it will be easier for them to believe in their own specialness.

If there's a specific aspect of themselves that your child finds hard to love and accept, seek out positive role models who share this characteristic. The more your child sees themselves reflected in the world, the less alone they'll feel. Knowing that you're not the only one to feel, think, or look the way you do is a huge relief and removes many barriers to self-worth.

The desire to fit in and be like their peers is strong at this age, so be gentle and let them work through this on their own terms. Try not to mock the fads or changing tastes that they buy into—remember how that felt when you were younger! Be yourself and let them be themselves, too, even if your child's choices don't always make sense to you.

I really hope you and your child have found this book useful. It's always hard when your child is struggling, and you're doing a great job by acknowledging their feelings and helping them build up their self-worth. On the next few pages, you'll find some suggestions for further reading and advice. Wishing you all the best of luck from one parent to another—your child is lucky to have you on their team!

Further advice

Occasional, short-term dips in self-worth aren't pleasant, but they are normal. However, if your child's sense of self-worth starts to interfere with their daily life then it's best to talk it through with their doctor.

Recommended reading

For parents and caregivers:
Mothers, Daughters, and Body Image: Learning to Love Ourselves as We Are
Hillary L. McBride
Post Hill Press, 2017

How to Talk so Kids Will Listen and Listen so Kids Will Talk
Adele Faber and Elaine Mazlish
Piccadilly Press, 2013

The Book You Wish Your Parents Had Read (and Your Children Will Be Glad That You Did)
Philippa Perry
Penguin, 2019

The Story Cure: An A–Z of Books to Keep Kids Happy, Healthy and Wise
Ella Berthoud and Susan Elderkin
Canongate, 2017

For kids:
You Are Awesome: Find Your Confidence and Dare to Be Brilliant at (Almost) Anything
Matthew Syed
Wren & Rook, 2018

Believing in Me: A Child's Guide to Self-Confidence and Self-Esteem
Poppy O'Neill
Sky Pony Press, 2019

Image credits

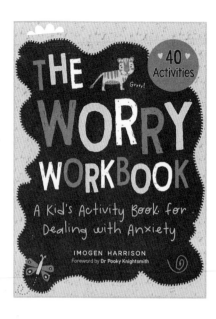

THE WORRY WORKBOOK

A Kid's Activity Book for Dealing with Anxiety

Imogen Harrison

Paperback

ISBN: 978-1-5107-6407-1

Worries come in all shapes and sizes and can creep up on us when we least expect them, stopping us from doing the things we really want and spoiling our fun. *The Worry Workbook* is here to help by explaining what worry is, offering creative ways to calm and distract yourself when worry strikes.

- ♥ Make a worry camera that captures fears and shrinks them into a manageable size.

- ♥ Color in a mood tracker that explores the rainbow of everyday emotions.

- ♥ Write on the magic mirror of compliments to help recognize your strengths.

- ♥ Create your very own list of anti-worry actions to fight fear and keep smiling.

Parents, this is for you: This book has been peer reviewed by a child psychologist, and there are explanations throughout just in case your child has questions about the activities.

BELIEVING IN ME
A Child's Guide to Self-Confidence
and Self-Esteem

Poppy O'Neill

Paperback

ISBN: 978-1-5107-4747-0

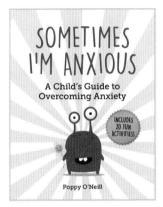

SOMETIMES I'M ANXIOUS
A Child's Guide to
Overcoming Anxiety

Poppy O'Neill

Paperback

ISBN: 978-1-5107-4748-7

I CAN BE BRAVE
A Child's Guide to Boosting
Self-Confidence

Poppy O'Neill

Paperback

ISBN: 978-1-5107-6408-8